the love i found

Charleston, SC
www.PalmettoPublishing.com

the love i found
Copyright © 2023 by Autumn Barnes

Hardcover ISBN: 979-8-8229-2844-2
Paperback ISBN: 979-8-8229-2845-9
eBook ISBN: 979-8-8229-2931-9

the love i found

AUTUMN BARNES

before you

i wasn't happy
but i wasn't unhappy.
i simply existed.

i had the same routine.
get up,
go to work,
come home.

maybe i'd hang out with my friends,
maybe i'd read a book,
maybe i'd just lay in bed and watch tv.

regardless of what i was doing,
i lived my life the way i wanted to,
and i was totally fine.

i was always the girl
everybody ran to
when everything was going downhill,
and falling apart.

i put everybody else first,
never once thinking
about what i needed.

and then
i met you.

during you

my days became happier.
i have something to look forward to.

you are everything to me.
i would do anything for you.
you are witty and smart,
goal oriented and focused.
you are the most handsome man i have ever met.
you make me feel safe.

priority.
more important than anything else.
when i see "time sensitive",
i know it's you.
even my phone knows
just how important you are.

when i envision my future,
you are in it.
you are my husband,
the father to my children.
i am your wife,
the mother to your children.

together, we create a home.
a healthy, loving environment.
we raise our children to be good people.
a lakehouse, a boat, jet skis.
everything we talked about.

but, at the end of the day,
it is all just a fantasy.
none of it is real,
and now i don't know if it ever will be.

i wished you were with me
every second of every day.
i wished you were with me
when i was with my friends.
i wished you were with me
when i was with my family.
i wished you were with me
when i was lonely.
i wished you were with me
when i wasn't.
i wished you were with me
in bed, watching movies.
i wished you were with me
when i woke up in the morning.
i missed you all the time.
you only missed me
when no one else was around.

i once told you
that every time i open up my heart,
it gets crushed.
you once told me,
that you would never do that to me.

and while that promise has already been broken,
i promise to keep this one.

i will love you in my life and death.
i will love you in this life and the next.
in this life,
my heart's purpose is you.
you are who my heart beats for.

we've been playing this game
for two years now.
saying "i miss you"
and running back.
this is my favorite game.

until i start second guessing.
the time you took to reply grew,
and the last time this happened,
there was someone else.

was everything you said a lie?
all the plans for our future,
every "i love you"
and every "i was made for you"?

now this is just a game
i don't want to play anymore.

the only thing you gave me
was more heartbreak.
more lies,
more excuses.
and yet, i became the monster.

i wasn't patient enough,
or attractive enough.
i wasn't the girl you wanted me to be.

i was the monster,
but all i did was love you.

loving you was the easiest thing
i have ever done.
and now, i realize,
that it will also be the hardest.

i was in a constant state of dread,
wishing i was full of despair.
i hated my internal war.
you were perfectly fine.

can you feel my uncertainty?
what about my heavy heart?
i can feel yours.
i listened and tried to pull you out.
you said nothing.
you carried on,
like i meant nothing.

i left the lights on
so you can find your way
back to me.
stop slipping through my fingers,
and just come home.

out of eight billion hearts,
i fell for the one
that does not beat for me.

i spent so many days
and so many nights
crying in my car,
feeling like my heart
was being ripped from my chest.
i knew i was slowly losing you.

your words told me
"stay", "everything is fine".
your actions told me
"run and never look back".

slowly i am coming to terms
with the fact that
i may have to let you go.

at first, i hated the idea.
i laid in bed every night
in tears, missing you,
and praying you would choose me.

now i lay in bed
and pray that you are happy.
of course i miss you.
of course i love you.

but at some point,
i have to choose myself.
i cannot choose
to keep living for you.

after you

Today is June 11.
The day I decided
to love me more.

I've started to enjoy the little things again.
I spend time with my friends,
and I actually enjoy myself.

I've become more comfortable
with being alone again.

I am learning to spread my love.
I'm learning to live my life without you.

I am so thankful for you.
But, in this moment,
I am more thankful for the lessons you taught.

I don't wait for you
to text me back.
I walk away from my phone.
I no longer wonder
where you are
or what you're doing.

I find myself
no longer thinking about you.
I don't wish you were with me
when I'm with my friends,
or my family.
I'm enjoying my life now.

And while I still have hope,
that it'll be me and you,
that hope has become smaller, and easier to carry.
With time, I think I'll be okay.

Deciding to go
was not an easy choice.
I hope our paths will cross again.
I cannot wait for you forever,
and I hope you understand.
I have to live my life.
I still have a lot of growing to do,
and I know you do too.

Maybe one day,
when we're who we're supposed to be,
we will meet again.
If not,
I will see you
in the next life.

About the Author

I am from Des Moines, Iowa. When I'm not writing, I am working as a daycare teacher, and I am also a photographer. Writing is a big part of my life. It's an escape for me, and becoming a published author has been a dream of mine since I was a little girl.

Milton Keynes UK
Ingram Content Group UK Ltd.
UKHW011823131023
430526UK00004B/255